STAUNCH ESSENCE

IT'S ALL LIFE.

SOUTRIK BHADRA

Copyright © Soutrik Bhadra
All Rights Reserved.

This book has been self-published with all reasonable efforts taken to make the material error-free by the author. No part of this book shall be used, reproduced in any manner whatsoever without written permission from the author, except in the case of brief quotations embodied in critical articles and reviews.

The Author of this book is solely responsible and liable for its content including but not limited to the views, representations, descriptions, statements, information, opinions and references ["Content"]. The Content of this book shall not constitute or be construed or deemed to reflect the opinion or expression of the Publisher or Editor. Neither the Publisher nor Editor endorse or approve the Content of this book or guarantee the reliability, accuracy or completeness of the Content published herein and do not make any representations or warranties of any kind, express or implied, including but not limited to the implied warranties of merchantability, fitness for a particular purpose. The Publisher and Editor shall not be liable whatsoever for any errors, omissions, whether such errors or omissions result from negligence, accident, or any other cause or claims for loss or damages of any kind, including without limitation, indirect or consequential loss or damage arising out of use, inability to use, or about the reliability, accuracy or sufficiency of the information contained in this book.

Made with ♥ on the Notion Press Platform
www.notionpress.com

Contents

Preface

I eagerly anticipate the opportunity to connect with you through the pages of this book. I hope that it will illuminate various aspects of my life, offering insights and reflections that resonate with you. As I share my journey, I am filled with excitement about the possibility of engaging in a meaningful conversation. This book is not just a collection of my experiences; it is an invitation for you to join me on this path of exploration and understanding. Together, we can delve into the lessons learned, the challenges faced, and the triumphs celebrated. I look forward to the dialogue that may arise from our shared experiences and perspectives, as we navigate the complexities of life together. Your thoughts and reflections are invaluable to me, and I am eager to hear how my story may connect with yours.

Prologue

This book chronicles my exploration of two of the most profound human emotions: love and pain. Through a series of personal experiences, I delve into their intricate connection and coexistence. My journey, marked by heartbreaks and setbacks, has revealed to me that every aspiration and notion we hold is fundamentally rooted in love, albeit expressed in various forms. This love can lead us to experience pain or, alternatively, unveil new dimensions of life. Our likes and dislikes, which shape our preferences, are deeply intertwined with the agile love we experience in connection with our emotions, life, and the people around us. Remember, don't complicate anything too much, it's all life.

Wild love

1. Those friends

It was nothing but friendship, they said.
Yes! It wasn't anything else but was the best.
It was out of those worldly messes and was the purest.

No heroic sacrifices!
No big help!
They still were the best.

Not doing anything.
Still!
Just being aside forever for each other for everything.
Until
the time became cunning.

2. Confession

You know, I love you.
But what I dislike is your unhappiness,
And, I hate your absence.
Life can be anything till it is you.
Infected me of you, never to be cured.
All have a world to live and a home to love.
I've both in you.

3. A lifetime is so less

The life you gave me,
I feel so blessed.
My life you are,
a lifetime seems so less.

Every moment I have with you,
I feel more for you.
As I am yours,
I live for you, I'll leave for you.

4. I & I

What is I? What is You?

It must be us but something new.

Their experiences themselves eliminated their experience of time.

Hours of conversation felt like moments of interaction.

The utterance of words was less.

Most of their communication was in silence.

So silent, so calming that they were in each other's breathing and hearts' beating.

Such was they, even irritated by the other also made their mood better.

Their just presence was enough for each other.

Is it us or just I?

I & I

What were they?

Were they lovers or friends?

Well, tags were limitations they didn't welcome because they weren't us.

Were they close to each other very much?

They weren't addicted or attached because they weren't us.

Was they in any relationship?

No, they couldn't start one or end one because they weren't us.

Just, I & I

'Us' separates but 'I' unites till it's eternal.

•7•

5. Being Love

Without the wish of the divine,
we would've never come across.
Beyond my own will, I am in love with you.
It was never an option and it will never be.
How did I start? How do I stop?
Not desperate to be with you but
just in the your love.
Can't really express what I've.
Not worth it like those royal princes
but I'm the loyal and pure one.
My life got 'you' flavoured during
your presence and during
your absence, I get lost in your memories.
Beyond time, living in the present and making an endless fall
towards the love
that will create memories for the future.
Offering my heart out and living in the clouds of love
knowing it will rain never but still trying to enjoy the
sunshine forever.
Flying towards you with my love without knowing the depth
I've already fallen for this stuff.
I know you don't need it but
Beyond my own will, I am in love with you.

It was never an option and it will never be.

6. Subtle Love

Beyond their will, they were in love.
No proposals but they were in love.
Never met each other but they were together.
Beyond them, they were for each other.

Hours they spend.
'Our's' they claimed.
All emotions criss-crossed them.
They turned into something they weren't.

They went so into each other that they went beyond each other.
Neither did the world understand nor they could make them understand.

What happened to them?
What did they become?
Separated they got or more together they got?

They went into a relationship but never proposed.
They were for each other but not together.
They broke up but they never were in a relationship.

Subtle love.

Intimate Despair

7. Burden of Pain

It takes courage to fall in love for the first time.

It takes trust to fall in love the next time.

I've the madness to fall everytime.

Only if it's you everytime

Us breaking makes me an orphan.

Maybe, it's the result of my sins of all time.

Pain doesn't stay forever.

It's the burden of pain.

I adore and carry the pain.

As her last gift........

8. Bloody Stains

I have hands with stains of blood.
Still, they are fresh, red and dark.
I close my eyes.
Still, I see red drops dripping.
They have forgiven, I've forgotten.
Still, I've those stains of blood.
I stand as a corpse.
Still, red blood drops.
Standing on my ashes.
Still, that dark memory flashes.
Fumes burn my soul.
Still, I have stains of blood.
Bleeding in sorrow and despair.
Still, I can't wash off those stains.
Standing under endless rain.
Still, I see those stains.

9. Vain

Life is haunting,
Struggle in breathing.
So tired,
I crave to be fired.
I wish to stop breathing, without even finishing whatever is left.
In the crowd of corpses.
I'm left to be ashes.
My breaths are the cost of my freedom.
So, let me go and never come back again.

10. Fossils of the scars

So many were the scars, like those countless stars.
Haunting like an old ghost makes me run till the end of life.
One day, I found myself.
It was enough to end the long dark night of my life.
All those scars became fossils within me.
Yes, the fossils of scars.

11. Dense!

In pain, fear, isolation,
I live, I leave.
Being that what I'm not,
Neither they nor I.
Are you?

Not really!
It's the depth of the moment that stole the moment itself.
Too much light made me blind, too much pain became bliss.
In the process of living, I left life itself.

Dense Life!
Bliss.

Embracing Life

12. In a twist of time

• 23 •

In a twist of time,
I became me but not mine.
In a twist of time,
I knew the flavours of life.
In a twist of time,
I was going to die.
In a twist of time,
I knew life.
That twist!
That time!
That life!

13. Losing affair

Once I'm lost,
they will know what I've lost.
My world is already lost,
I'm lost in the world.

14. Always a Ploy

All of me is a ploy.
Garnering all that's life,
Finding the path to death.
All of me is a ploy.
Reticent about my plans,
I walk in the crowd as sacrosanct.
All of me is a ploy.

15. Those heroes

The opulence of ignorance finds arbitrary expression.

Misers don't spend senses to afford life.

World engulfed in enslavement to the enchantment of entertainment.

Everything results in an iteration of illusion.

All the big circles look like straight paths.

All were born heroes but are now villains to themselves.

16. Wayward

Entitled insanity camouflages stupidity.
Pragmatic minds being the hopeless maverick.
Obsession of validity restraints vitality.
Entice the pursuit of the enigmatic.
Blurry eyes of the world incapacitate reality.
Unfortunate life has lost the gift of magic.
Clarity that perceives the silent calamity.
Unfolding with time the effortless tragic.
Unavailable human beings with humanity.

17. The Shine of the last time

Lost in the shine of darkness.
Hold my hands, get me in your arms.
Find me in the corner of the light,
show me the shadow of mine.

Hey, am I lost or have I found it?
Get me to the end of time.
Find me for the last time,
I'm yours and you will be mine.

Our perception of love is often limited to romantic notions, and we tend to equate intimacy solely with physical connections. However, we must recognize that love is not merely an action or a practice; it is a conscious choice that can thrive in any circumstance or relationship. To truly embrace love, you must commit to it wholeheartedly. While relationships require effort beyond just love, nothing meaningful can flourish without that foundational feeling. Never love yourself more than you love your ones and never love them more than you love yourself, be fair with love. The more you communicate, the more you understand, and that builds trust. Never hesitate to go for the love you deserve. Good luck to you in love, and may you experience and express as much as love possible in life.